ECOMMERCE
2020 & BEYOND

ECOMMERCE 2020 & BEYOND

DROPSHIPPING, RETAIL ARBITRAGE, SEO, SOCIAL MEDIA MARKETING & MORE

Marc Stanford

ECOMMERCE 2020 & BEYOND

MARC STANFORD
amazon.com/author/marcstanford

Printed in the United States of America
First Printing: November 2019
ISBN-13: 9781705601433

Imprint: Independently published
Cover designed by pro_ebookcovers, FL, USA

To all who have the vision, and the dedication
to become financially independent by establishing
an eCommerce business

CONTENTS

INTRODUCTION   1
THE FUNDAMENTALS OF ECOMMERCE   2
THE ECOMMERCE CHECKLIST   5
SUCCESSFUL SELLING ON POPULAR PORTALS   9
PASSIVE INCOME OPTION   17
OPTIMIZING YOUR ADS   24
THRIVING ECOMMERCE MODELS   32
CONCLUSIONS   37

ABOUT THE AUTHOR   39

"A diamond is a chunk of coal that did well under pressure."
-Henry Kissinger

INTRODUCTION

I n today's rapidly changing times where more and more people are moving towards entrepreneurship, intending to start their own business and trying to change their future for the better, the Internet has created ample opportunities. Through the reach and access to the Internet, it has become easier to achieve the goal of being ones' own boss. Nowadays, eCommerce is one of the most lucrative options that can generate high revenues, but starting a successful eCommerce business involves quite complicating initial steps that might scare beginners.

Sometimes it can be overwhelming to get understandable and easy-to-apply answers to difficult questions related to eCommerce, such as: "How to start an online business store? How to prepare a market strategy for the business? Where to sell the products? How to sell products and build a brand? How to differentiate from competitors' offerings and gain the trust of customers? How are payments processed?" and the list goes on and on.

ECommerce is growing day by day. According to the studies performed by the digital business research site eMarketer, the eCommerce industry is growing annually with more than twenty percent, and the total sales volume of eCommerce will reach up to $27 trillion by 2020. Ecommerce is supposed to show steady growth, that is why it is never too late to start an online business. However, as in any other business, it is vital to know all the pros and cons of the eCommerce industry before establishing a new online company.

"ECommerce 2020 & Beyond" is written to provide the readers with all necessary information, essential to become successful in the highly competitive arena of eCommerce. In this book, the author digs deep into the eCommerce industry and endeavors to cover all significant aspects of this exciting field of business, which is full of opportunities but also traps. In addition to the professional advice necessary to start and run a successful eCommerce business, this book shows you ways for a detailed and straight forward approach towards customers, suppliers, competitors, and also an analysis of the fast-changing effects of globalization on online businesses.

THE FUNDAMENTALS OF ECOMMERCE

ECommerce, also referred to as online or internet commerce, is the broad term used for describing the process of buying and selling products and services, and the transfer of money as well as data to perform these transactions. The term encompasses any commercial transaction facilitated through the internet.

On the other hand, eBusiness, or electronic business, can be described as the administration of conducting all possible types of business activities via the internet, including providing essential services to the customers and communicating with all stakeholders. Since eBusiness, along with buying and selling products, also covers fields like customer support, remote technical analysis, and trouble-shooting, eCommerce is considered a subsystem of eBusiness.

ECommerce officially began with a small incident dated back in 1994, when a CD by Sting was sold via a website named *NetMarket*, which was an American retail platform. It was the first occasion in history when a customer purchased a product with the use of the internet from an online seller. Ever since then, the process of buying and selling goods has become easier on eCommerce websites. Regardless if they are small businesses, large corporations, or freelancers, eCommerce is beneficial for all types of sellers, enabling them to target customers on a global scale, which was almost impossible earlier. In direct relation to this trend, the global eCommerce markets started to expand rapidly, and there is no end in sight!

According to a study conducted by the Gartner Group in June 2019 covering the largest national markets, the world's five largest eCommerce markets are:
1) China: $672 billion in annual online sales, accounting for sixteen percent of total Chines retail sales. With an impressive thirty-five percent annual growth, China is also the world's fastest-growing eCommerce market.
2) United States: $340 billion in annual online sales, which is eight percent of total American retail sales.
3) United Kingdom: $99 billion in sales annually, accounting for a decent fifteen percent of total British retail sales.
4) Japan: $79 billion in annual eCommerce sales, which stands for five point five percent of total retail sales.
5) Germany: $73 billion in annual e-sales, with an 8.4% share of total retail sales.

Types of ECommerce Models

Models for eCommerce business can be classified into the following types:

> Business to Consumer (B2C)

According to this model, an online retailer sells its products to the end-user directly; e.g., a customer buys a mobile phone from an online retail store.

> ➤ Business to Business (B2B)

This model can be described as buying and selling goods or services taking place between two businesses; e.g., a company purchases software support as a service from another company.

> ➤ Consumer to Consumer (C2C)

It can be defined as a business transaction between two consumers, who can trade with each other in an online environment; a private person – not a company - sells his or her collection of records to another consumer.

> ➤ Consumer to Business (C2B):

This model describes business happening between a consumer who sells his or her goods or services to a business organization, e.g., digital influencer advertisements for a product manufactured by a company.

Examples of ECommerce

ECommerce can be further split into many forms based on the types of transactions happening between two parties.

- Retail

Selling of the products by a business to an end-user directly without any chain in between.

- Wholesale

Selling of goods in bulk to the retailers.

- Dropshipping

Products are manufactured by a company and shipped directly to the end-user on behalf of company, usually a retailer.

- Crowdfunding

Process of funding the launch of a new product or financing a startup company by a group of several small investors.

- Subscription

Automatic selling of a product or a service to a customer regularly until the consumer unsubscribes the service.

- Physical products

Goods that are manufactured, stored as an inventory, and shipped to the customers when they purchase it.

- Digital products

Products that can be digitally downloaded by the consumers, like software, images, music and video, courses, templates, or any other media files.

- Services

Skills that are provided by a company, e.g., customer support, or a freelancer, e.g. graphic design, in exchange for money.

As already pointed out, eCommerce is the fastest-growing area of business, supercharged by innovations in technology and changing consumer behavior. Super-fast, broadband internet, the world wide web, social media, user-friendly websites, secure online payment options, ultrahigh download speed, smartphones, and tablets changed our daily lives and transformed our habits. Today an increasing number of people are choosing to shop online, as well as to be online, instead of going to a mall and meeting with friends face-to-face.

The universal market forces for any business transaction are supply and demand. These forces apply to any type of business globally, but especially for eCommerce, the internet creates continuously expanding opportunities.

The following guiding principles are responsible for leading to success in eCommerce:

- The two basic equations to understand online sales is:

[Total number of visitors x Conversion rate x Average order value] = Total value of sales
[Purchasing customers / Total number of visitors] = Conversion rate

To increase sales, only three parameters need to be modified; understandably, either the number of visitors, or the conversion rate, or the average order value needs to be increased. Customer satisfaction leads to returning customers and to repeat-business. Repeat-business transforms *average order value* to *customer lifetime value*, which increases another essential parameter, namely *retention*.

- These three key strategic areas of eCommerce must remain in focus: *Traffic* (number of visitors), *Conversion* (number of buying visitors), and *Retention* (number of loyal, returning customers).

- The four pillars of any successful eCommerce business are:
Technology: user-friendly, secure, reliable, multi-language & -currency
Customers: targeting acquisition, conversion, and retention, 24/7 service
Product: quality, competitive price, brand, unique features, information
Investment: in production, people, marketing, sales, after-sales support.

THE ECOMMERCE CHECKLIST

To start an eCommerce business, one needs to have a proper plan and strategy. You have to come up with a business plan, and necessary financial resources, and of course, an adequate social media marketing strategy. It is also a good idea to study some real-world examples to get a thorough knowledge of the field and to learn from the mistakes of others.

Let's have a look at some of the critical points, which you need to follow if you want to establish a new eCommerce business successfully.

> SMART Objectives

To achieve success in the eCommerce industry, you need to create SMART goals. SMART goals are specific, measurable, attainable, relevant, and time-bound. These goals are achievable because they consist of clearly defined work-packages without grey areas. So why should you apply SMART goals to your working and even personal life? Not only because it's such a satisfying feeling to tick something off your 'to-do' list, but they can help you become more organized and sort out your priorities. These kinds of goals are highly motivating and can give a sense of focus and purpose.

> Business name and store name

While choosing a name for your eCommerce store, you should aim to have a short and simple name, which is easy for your customers to remember. Additional benefits are linked with names, which have a meaning in several languages. One of the most important things that you should keep in mind is that your store name should be unique. It shouldn't be already available on www or any social media platform; otherwise, you will most likely face copyright problems.

> Web Hosting

Web hosting is one of the crucial ingredients to start an eCommerce website. Web hosting software can be classified into further two types for building an eCommerce website.
1) Hosted eCommerce software, e.g., Shopify, BigCommerce, Wix and Volusion.
2) Self-hosted open-source eCommerce software, e.g., WooCommerce, Magento, OpenCart and PrestaShop.

> Domain Names

A domain name is the identification of the website. The domain extension of every country is different like, .uk is for the United Kingdom, .jp is for Japan, and so on. Therefore, you should either choose a particular domain to target a particular country's audience or generic domains such as .com for a global approach and serving international customers worldwide. A few important points to consider while choosing a domain name are:
- it should be short and not too complicated,
- it should be easy to remember,

- it should match or represent your brand,
- it shouldn't have a dash or hyphen, and no special characters.

> ➤ Consider the Platform Where to Build Your Store

There are several eCommerce stores builder available in the market. But before you approach them, it's better to know what your priorities or functionalities are, which you want in your eCommerce store. Some of the critical metrics are price, available features, support, ease of use, and performance.

> ➤ Know the Best Commercial Model for Your Business

Models for eCommerce business were briefly explained in the previous chapter. Below is a more detailed description.

- B2C - Business to Consumer

As the name itself suggests, the B2C- business model is the model under which the business sells its products or services directly to the consumers. As it directly sells to the consumer without taking the help of any intermediary, it is a much shorter process and, therefore, faster than the B2B model. For example, if a consumer goes to a shop to purchase a handbag, it will be a straightforward transaction as compared to a situation when a company imports goods from another company, for example, from a manufacturer. Therefore, B2C is less expensive as compared to the B2B business. Many B2C businesses are using digital marketing to connect with their customers directly.

- B2B - Business to Business

According to the B2B model, a business sells its products or services to another business. Most of the time, a business is the end-user, for example, when a company purchases a licensed software from another company. In a situation when a wholesaler sells products in bulk to a retailer, which further sells these products to a consumer, the consumer becomes the end-user. Therefore, the business cycle of B2B sales is usually longer than B2C.

- C2B - Consumer to Business

C2B is the exact opposite of B2C. In this type of transaction model, the consumer can sell products or services to businesses directly. Many freelance websites, like Freelancer, Fiverr, Guru, and Upwork – the pioneer in this field - are the best examples of it. This model of eCommerce allows consumers to put a price tag on their services and rate their product. Nowadays, even consumers/freelancers have started to advertise their products/services with the help of digital media influencers.

- C2C - Consumer to Consumer

C2C allows one consumer to sell their goods or services to another consumer; for example, a person sells old furniture to a consumer with the help of advertisements on local newspapers or an eCommerce website. Besides consumers, many eCommerce websites also act as consumers and work on this business model, too. This type of eCommerce business model comes with attached risks, such as payment security and quality assurance. Since the business is happening between two consumers, it is challenging to keep a check on quality control and ensure safe payment. The option of returning the purchased good is not always possible.

> ➤ Define your target market

For being able to run a successful eCommerce store consistently, it is essential to identify your target audience.

When you are connected to your targeted audience, it is easy for you to sell your product more easily and quickly because your website will start getting more genuine traffic. For example, your eCommerce store is selling fashion-related materials, and you are targeting an audience who wants to purchase electronic items. In such a case, it will be difficult for you to increase the genuine audience for your brand. But if you can connect with your target market, you will also be able to increase your ROI, which can also give a boost to your sales.

> ➢ Evaluate who your competitors are

To excel in business, it is vital to study your competitors deeply. Since the use of increased to a thousand folds, therefore the competition in eCommerce business has also increased. Well, the basic idea is that you should come up with a unique proposition by observing your competitors' successes and failures. This exercise helps you in finding your potential customers, which in turn will help you to increase your business. Try to implement new ideas into the business which your competitors aren't doing.

> ➢ Examine Both Demographics and Psychographics

For identifying your target customers, it is imperative to involve technology in your due diligence process. With the help of a detailed study of the data regarding the customers you are aiming at, it is much easier for you to form a business strategy. Therefore, try to use demographics and psychographics. Demographics refers to the study of the population, which gives you information about a person's age, gender, and occupation, while psychographics provides information regarding a person's behavior, which is useful to analyze whether a person will make a purchase or not.

> ➢ Choose the Manufacturer for Your Wholesale Products

To create trust between you and your potential customers, it is very important to select a proper manufacturer and wholesaler. Therefore, you need to select those wholesalers who offer you quality guarantees, on-time delivery, and a variety of products, which helps you in increasing your business. It is recommended to do thorough research on Google or AliBaba.com to find genuine manufacturers and vendors. This is an excellent solution; in fact, the majority of Amazon FBA (Fulfillment by Amazon) vendors source products from China and serve the US and European consumers with these imported goods.

> ➢ Mark up your products

One of the essential points to keep in mind to get more sales on your eCommerce store is to keep competitive prices for your products. At the launch of your product, you are penetrating an established market. If the prices of your new-comer products are higher than the established competitor's products in this market niche, customers will not purchase them. Likewise, if the prices of your products are too low, potential buyers will have doubts about the quality of the products. In such a case, you would be facing a problem even to achieve break-even in your business.

> ➢ Make use of Outsourcing

If the business starts running, then you cannot continue doing everything on your own. To achieve success in the field of eCommerce, you need to work in a team, or you can outsource your projects. Outsourcing will not only unburden you but also enable you to address your customer's high demands. While outsourcing your eCommerce work to some extent, emphasize hiring real professionals and experts, so that you can give your customers an excellent service.

> Plan your Social Media Strategy

In today's rapidly changing digital world, you need to market your eCommerce store on various digital media platforms, like Facebook, Twitter, Instagram, and LinkedIn. Google Ads, Facebook Ads, Amazon PPC (Pay for Click), and LinkedIn Sponsored Ads to help you to reach out to your potential customers. Therefore, to increase your business, you must plan a proper digital marketing strategy and reserve a sufficient marketing budget. This strategy will increase your businesses' visibility, lift your search engine rank, and build trust in your customers towards you.

SUCCESSFUL SELLING ON POPULAR PORTALS

Selling products online is unique because of the massive range of customers you can reach, but remember, the millions of potential customers are also targeted by possibly thousands of competitor websites. For successful selling, you first have to drive traffic to your site, then deliver exceptional service and excellent products. The good news is, your overhead cost selling products online is significantly lower than opening a physical store. Things will probably move slowly as you are first getting started, but the more time and effort you put into creating and promoting your online store, the more sales you will see. Keep in mind that you will need to build multiple channels for marketing your products. Social media, content, search engine optimization (SEO), and paid advertising all take time, tweaking, and a little bit of work every day.

Considering and carefully selecting the market niche, which you want to target is vital to the success of your business. Smaller niches will have less competition, giving you a better chance of connecting with potential buyers. On the other hand, your pool of customers will be smaller. Spend some time thinking about your niche and balancing the level of competition with the size of the market. Keep in mind that digital products like software, music, and eBooks can be sold internationally and delivered instantly, and thus have a different cost structure in comparison with selling physical products. If you sell digital products, the delivery should be automated. If you sell physical products, prompt shipping is important, as is providing the buyer with the ability to track their shipment.

Visitors to your website or blog tend to have a short attention span, so you generally have about 10 seconds to grab their attention when they first land on your page. Don't put obstacles in their way or make them overthink. Many visitors will leave your site the moment they hit a snag.

Therefore, don't force visitors to register when they first visit your website. Also, don't make the navigation on your website or blog complicated to use. Equally important, don't make the buying process long and don't try to collect more than necessary personal information from buyers. The more steps and information requested, the higher the friction, and the more sales you will lose as buyers abandon their purchase.

Show potential customers that your site is secure and verified by trusted third parties like Symantec or McAfee. If you are planning on handling credit card information, your website or blog needs to be on a secure server and compliant with the Security Standards Council (PCI) rules.

And finally, promote your online store. You need to attract people to your store and help them take the step of making a purchase. Try writing relevant articles or blog posts on your site, or finding guest posting opportunities on other websites that your prospective customers visit. Get other people to review your products on their website. The techniques to help your website appear higher in search results are SEO. This process has spawned a whole industry on its own.

Becoming a successful seller on eBay

If you want to start an eCommerce business without your eCommerce website, then eBay could be the best option for you. It doesn't matter whether you want to sell your products in small or large quantities or you have your own manufactured or new items, eBay can become your savior to reach out to more and more customers. If you want to become successful on eBay, follow these seven steps.

1) Product Photos

For a high sales rate of your products; it is recommended to list your eBay products with professionally shot and excellent quality photographs. The images should be taken from every possible angle enabling customers to have a satisfactory look at the product before purchasing it.

There are a few guidelines of eBay which should be followed to make a listing. A picture should have a minimum of 500 pixels, it should not contain any border, artwork, text, or any seller's logo. eBay offers its watermark service, or you may create it yourself. If you are listing brand new items, then you can upload stock pictures.

2) Product Research

You must do proper research on your product before you do the listing. This research process should include efforts to find a competitive price in comparison with the other sellers listing that same product. The outcome of this research gives you an idea of its market value. To get more insight on this subject, it is a good idea to subscribe to eBay's Listing Analytics. This free subscription allows you to review key metrics of your listings and see how your listings are performing. These metrics are rank, format, impressions, clicks, click-throughs, sold items, sell-through, watchers, and sales. Keeping an eye on these metrics makes you a more effective seller on eBay.

Further benefits of Listing Analytics are access to a detailed study about various essential points like best selling items on eBay, the trend of a particular product, and its performance on the website. Apart from all these, you can also take a reference from the auctions in which you can set a reserve price for your products. In case your item cannot be sold in the auction, you still have to pay four percent of the reserve price as a cost of listing.

3) Shipping Options

eBay also provides a wide range of shipping options. You can either ship the products from your side or make use of Dropshipping, namely asking the manufacturer to send the product directly to your customers' addresses on your behalf. It is a good option if you choose the eBay shipping method, which suits your location and the type of product which you are selling. After selecting the shipping method, you should also include the shipping cost to your product, as well.

If you want to regain your customers, it is vital to pack your products efficiently and deliver them on time. This helps you in building a trustworthy relationship with your customers. A person will not buy a product next time if the received parcel is shabbily packed, and the product is damaged due to this reason. You should take care of every step of the packaging process.

4)   Product Descriptions

It is essential to have a perfect listing to become a successful seller on eBay. In March 2019, eBay changed the listing rules and increased the number of free sales significantly from twenty to one-thousand a month. While this may seem like a dream come true for sellers, keep in mind that the highest cost when selling on eBay is usually the *final value fee*, rather than the *listing fee*. eBay takes ten percent of the sales price of any item you successfully sell, including postage, and you'll pay extra if your buyer pays via PayPal, so be sure to factor these costs in. eBay has a selling tab in the *My eBay* section at the top right corner under which you can see the number of free listings that are left.

Before you make a listing, it is highly recommended to do thorough research of your product, so that after the listing of your product, it becomes easy for the potential customers to search, and find it via a search engine. Apart from all these, you should also pay attention to mentioning the key details of your product; this creates additional benefits for you as it gives your potential customers more insight into your product and your online store.

5)   Payment Options

It is more beneficial for you if you offer multiple payment options to your customers, which will not only make it easier for them to buy your product, but it also helps to boost your business volume. You can accept the payment against your product via debit cards, credit cards, PayPal, and cash on delivery (COD). This increases your popularity amongst the customers.

In some of the categories, eBay also alternative payment options, such as allows checks and bank to bank transfers. But to make your product sales process successful, you should be able to make a better judgment in selecting the payment method.

6)   Earning Feedback

One of the best ways through which your sales can increase organically is via customers' feedback on your products. The number of positive feedbacks received on your products have a very positive impact on your future sales. Potential customers prefer to buy from a seller who offers products with high quality with many positive feedbacks.

If you are new to this business, then you should bid your products at a competitive price i.e., not too low and not too high. This pricing strategy helps you to building a trust-based relationship with your customers. You should also keep the quantity of the different products in your portfolio limited so that you can focus on those key products and meet the need of your customers in terms of information, support, and service. When you fully understand the process, and the business eventually improves, you can increase the price of your products gradually and add new products to your portfolio.

7) Professionalism

If you can maintain a professional behavior towards your customers, then success is almost guaranteed in this business. Make sure that the customers should not face any problem caused by your side. Provide them with the best customer service to increase customer satisfaction, which will helps you in increasing your sales. Deliver products to them at the right time. Give your customers the best service, and they will keep coming back to your store.

Selling successfully through Shopify

Ever since its first appearance in 2004, Shopify has upgraded itself from being small snowboarding gear shop to the biggest shopfront handling forum around the world. At present, more than six hundred thousand merchants use Shopify to operate their businesses online. The software of Shopify is intricate enough to satisfy expert dealers and settled businesses. It is also very easy-to-use so that commoners can give their business a quick launch and earn additional revenue. These characteristics create the so-called *Charm of Shopify.*

Many people, these days, are acquainted with the fact that creating an enterprise has become way more manageable. Though, there is a hike in the competition because of fewer blockages at the entrance of this online-world; this can slow down the income flow. You are not alone if you face challenges at online retail platforms; many people go through the same regularly. This fact leads various dealers to the dilemma of having no clue why consumers are not buying their products.

Here are nine key points you need to consider for becoming successful Sn Shopify.

1) Make your Shop Mobile

Until a few years back, the major part of the online traffic was brought in by desktop computers. However, this scenario has changed. In the third-largest continent, North America, more than sixty percent of net consumption is done via tablets, smartphones, and similar gizmos. Europe is following this trend. Led by China and Japan, this change in consumer buying behavior is even more advanced in Asia. This proves that more than half of internet usage is done from mobile gadgets. By not having a mobile application fundamentally means that you have already lost half of your sales and interaction chances; by not engaging your visitors.

Having an app can unlock the door for plenty of visitors to get involved with your store with proffering additional advantages:
- Odds of visitors bouncing away are less on mobile gizmos.
- Sales will be driven to mobile devices.
- Customer experience and feedback will improve; they can send products to their carts on phones and then later purchase it through their desktops.
- When it comes to mobile inquiries, your store can have its rank on the Google search listing.
- Shopify provides a responsive checkout option so that the users can change to their choice of devices.

- If you have paid for ads, you can keep a check on the reaction of mobile users rather than excluding them.

In the world of the increasing domination of mobile devices on human lives, this small step can prove to be worthy of leading your store to success. You can sell your products after getting your app(s) optimized, and the later choices you make leave an impact on your triumph.

2) Trading more Goods

This pointer might sound simple but is very accurate, indeed. If one wishes to make more income, then they have to sell a wider variety of products. This strategy is evident and poles apart from being new. Moreover, in the early years, the retail giant Amazon used this selling strategy to beat the established physical book shops, like Barnes & Noble. To get started, you need to cautiously go through the available options and ensuring that you are pliant with the product range. You do not have to limit yourself; instead, pick the options which are germane to your brand. Having a more comprehensive product range can assist better categorization to attract more traffic via SEO as well. The utmost work to be done is to discuss and search on product grouping and the products that can be sent out for gratis to please your customers.

Here are a few methods to view what products are increasing retailer gains:
- Go through Amazon and arrange by reviews; this can lead your search party to some of the most indistinct products. Search for these product categories on Goggle, and you can check what comes first in the shopping tabs and ads. This is a steady path for success.
- Create dummy accounts; visit stores that are similar to your store and your brand; check what ads show up on your newsfeed. With the gained insight, promote your products in a similar way, and your offerings can make their way to popularity and high demand.
- Rummage through the top traders of products from your category on sites like eBay, and Amazon.

3) Retention of Customers

The recorded data states that approximately sixty-five percent of the total sales globally show up from returning clients. This information points out that resources spent on retaining these customers and increasing their standard expenditure are comparatively economical than attaining new clienteles.

Think about how trustworthy are the old sellers to buy form in contrast to putting faith in someone new. Customer retention can show drastic improvements in your brand progress and profit growth graph; hence, it is necessary. A study performed by the management consulting company Bain & Company states that an improvement in customer retention by five percent can increase the profit margin by seventy-five percent. Also, almost all flourishing businesses apportion their resources for consumer retention as against the unsuccessful ones.

To simplify, for expanding your Shopify store, you must know how to retain your clients. If you lose your customers, then you have to put in efforts to get new clientele and function harder to upkeep the income. For the prevention of this and similar occurrences, you have to take quick and dynamic precautions for guaranteed consumer retention. Below listed are a few steps for efficient retention.

- Steady Email communication

You can send emails to your customers regularly. This routine keeps the clients committed, and ensures that the customers recall your brand first when they are looking for any product. The many motives behind mailing include: notifying for the availability of a new product range, advertising offers and sales, seasonal mails, and of course, wishing well on the particular dates of the clients, as well as for holidays and celebrations like Thanksgiving, Christmas, New Year's Eve.

- Surprise and Satisfy consumers

You should try and reach over and above for all your customers. A few times, a little generous thought can make a significant contribution. One way to do this is to send handwritten notes and small letters to the customers and buyers.

- Upgrade the Packaging

Nobody likes to see their product delivered in lousy packaging. Therefore, put your efforts into personalizing and customizing your packaging materials. Just like Apple puts in detailed hard work to make the unboxing of their products phenomenal for buyers. Share your products with related YouTube channels and ask them if they can unbox a few of your products on their videos. Place handwritten notes in the packaging. Place offers and sale coupons, discount vouchers on their next orders. Place gift coupons and vouchers so that they can share it with their next of kin and friends. Pack manuals wherever needed. Try out something new with the packaging, something that brings a smile on customers' faces.

- Notifications on Cart Abandonment

People sometimes get interrupted while placing their orders due to other work or network issues. Generally, these sale transactions are lost because the replacement of the order slips from the mind of the user. You can remind them to retrieve their product selection with the abandonment email.

- Refocusing

Refocusing is a stealthy and even cunning way of securing customer retention. This method plants a cookie in customers' browsers, which stores the data of the products they were going through. The cookie later ensures the display of earlier browsed products again via Facebook ads or Google ads to gain their attention back.

- Birthday mails

Everyone loves to get wished well on their birthday; so do your customers. You can add on to their celebration by giving them exclusive offer coupons and vouchers. You can further assist them with a platform, which happens to be your store, to use that coupon.

- Repeat Buyer Discount

The best way to retain your customers is to engage them with your special offers. This habit increases the traffic in your store, which in turn also helps in increasing your sales. To attract more customers to your Shopify store you should also put frequent discounts on your products. Discount campaigns play a vital role in building a trustworthy relationship between you and your customers.

- Create a Loyalty Program

Another meaningful way through which you can increase your customer retention is by gifting points to your returning customers, which inculcates a sense of reward in them for their loyalty. This method not only helps you enhance your sales volume, but it also increases your customer's loyalty towards you.

4) Curate Product Reviews

Customers' feedback is one of the essential ways through which you can increase your business's revenue. Just like any eCommerce website, the customers' reviews play an important role in increasing or decreasing a particular product's sales in the same way the feedback of other people inspires a customer to buy a particular product or not. Therefore, encourage your customers to give honest feedback about their purchases from your store; it is highly beneficial for your business.

5) Be Responsive to Social Media

Create a social media page for your Shopify account and also reply to the feedbacks of the customers; this correspondence also helps you increase your sales. Plus, this is an added benefit to you as customers love to have one-on-one communication in case they are facing any problem with their newly purchased product. It also shows how dedicated you are to your customers.

6) Don't Take Complaints Personally

Take care of your customers, listen to their remarks about your products. It will not only help you in increasing your sales but also help you in retaining your customers. Try to communicate with them via social media platforms, because if you don't pay any heed to their query, it can give you and your store bad ratings and negative publicity. If you provide your customers with the best quality services, it will also positively increase your business.

7) Build an Email List

Apart from all these, you can also choose one more way to engage your customers, and that is maintaining an email list. In this way, you can directly send emails to your customers and inform them about new product launches, the latest offers, and discounts on your Shopify store. These regular emails can improve your store's traffic and also reduce your dependence on other social media platforms.

Therefore, email marketing is one of the best ways to increase your business, and it also creates awareness among people about your store. The US email marketing service Mailchimp is recommended to establish and maintain your promoting activities via email.

8) Optimize Your Content for Ecommerce

Content marketing is one of the best ways to advertise your products. It helps you promoting not only your specific brand but also your Shopify store to a great extent. In content marketing, you can also share your services and products on other social media platforms, as well. Content marketing can increase the revenue of your Shopify store up to eight times as compared to traditional marketing methods. In an eCommerce store, there is a wide range of possibilities for content marketing so that your Shopify store revenue can increase rapidly.

- Video Content

If you can put a relevant video regarding your Shopify store and your catalog of products, then it helps your customers in making better purchase choices. Such a video feature is beneficial for you, too, as it can increase your sales to a great extent.

- Product Descriptions

If you can describe the qualities of your product in great detail, then you can increase not only the sales of this particular product but also the traffic on the website through SEO.

- Images

Apart from the product description, images also play an essential part in content marketing. When a customer can see the clear images of the product, his or her trust over the company increases. The images you display should be of outstanding quality.

9) Contest Marketing

If you want to pour some excitement into your customers, then contest marketing can help you out in this scenario. When you organize a contest on your social media pages and encourage your customers to engage in it, it has the potential to increase the traffic on your store, and the sales of your products, as well.

Besides, the contest can help you in generating the leads for your store. When you organize a contest, your potential and loyal customers can get a chance to win some prizes. Contests can help you grow your target audience and also help you increase your business; hence, this marketing concept is widely considered an excellent way to attract customers. Such a contest also generates valuable leads for your store.

PASSIVE INCOME OPTION

Passive income is technically an income you receive on a regularly that involves little effort on your part. You get paid every month or year but don't participate in the management or contribute work in the investment. Few investments offer actual passive income streams, most usually involve some level of ongoing work to make money. In the past, success with an online store meant you needed your products or some strategy to buy and sell used products. Now you don't even have to do that. By selling affiliate products, you don't even need to create something of your own to sell. Just post a picture and a link of a product and let the money roll in, right? Not quite!

The reality of an online store is that they are easy to set up, but success takes a bit more work. Your online store is likely to provide even less passive income than blogging. Online stores aren't a good source of passive income because they are only the distribution channel for your or someone else's products. An online store is only the way you get your products or your affiliate products in front of potential customers. The online store itself makes no money.

This income option is different from some of the real passive income sources like stocks, bonds, and some forms of real estate investment. These investments increase in value without any effort on your part – the definition of passive income. With an online store, you'll always need to be managing your e-commerce site to grow traffic and find new products to sell. That can be a very profitable business but it's certainly not passive. Nevertheless, there are options to make money with eCommerce, which at least create the impression of generating passive income. Here are a few:

Blogging

A few years ago, blogging was considered as another pastime work that was done by a few people along with their regular jobs. But at present, writing blogs has changed. In 2019, blog writing emerged as a lucrative online occupation, and the people in large numbers started creating blogs for entering this noble profession. Much like other occupations, there are different stages of blog writing with earnings ranging from $1,000 to $2 million annually.

The amount of money you can make by writing blogs depends on factors like:
The type of métier and topics you choose,
The amount of time you spend on acquiring knowledge and its execution,
The amount of traffic your blog attracts, and
The type of digital marketing features you use.

Also, factors like consistency, networking, self-motivation, and targets play an important role in enhancing your skills. Your digital promotion abilities can assist in rapid growth in the digital blogging scene.

There are several ways by which you can use your blogs for monetary purposes. All of this is solely based on the blogging standard of a person and the type of blog they write; you can choose the genre you like, and that corresponds to your interests.

> Ad Networks

One of the easiest and frequently used methods for monetizing a blog post is by using Ad Networks. Two of the most famous Ad Networks are Google AdSense and Media.net. But firstly, you must have a blog to avail of these services. They put up ads automatically depending upon the content of your article and user interest and browsing history. Many new blog creations utilize these approaches to monetize; because they generate periodic income.

If your blog posts get lower than 300 views each day, then you can use some other known ad networks, although, your primary focus should always be on getting acceptance by Google AdSense and Media.net - the earlier, the better. Also, if you use contextual ad methods and do not make enough income, you can try switching to direct advertisements or affiliate advertisements.

> Direct Advertisements

There is no cross-questioning about Google AdSense being the first advertisement program for all the bloggers, but it sure has a few restrictions. One of the more significant constraints is that you get paid according to the amount per click.

If you can seize up direct advertisements, you can substitute the AdSense units with the direct ad ones. By using different networks and inserting a page on your blog titled "Media-kit" or "Advertise with us" you can grab new agreements; these are some of the best paths to start direct advertisements. You can also employ plug-ins like *WPAdvancedAds* to handle the advertisements. The ideal method to do this is by creating an adept email ID and using Google applications.

> Affiliate Marketing

Affiliated ads are the other best option to go for if you wish to make money online; a single sale can make you comparatively more money than a sole click on popup ads. This option is being heavily used by the bloggers these days and one of the most lucrative ones indeed. The most popular affiliate marketplaces that you can choose from are ClickBank, Awin, Amazon Affiliate Program, PartnerStack, CJ (Commission Junction) Affiliate, ImpactRadius, and ShareASale.

One other perk of affiliate marketing is that it can be used on any blogging forum like Wix, Medium, Squarespace, and even LinkedIn. Sharing the unique affiliate link can help you earn a big part of the sale amount. For this, you only have to recommend the product via its affiliate link, and when someone purchases the product, you receive your share of the sale amount. Currently, affiliate marketing is the primary source of income for bloggers worldwide.

> Native Advertising

Native Advertising has always been the center of attraction in money-making from blogging because it matches the form and function of the platform upon which it appears. In particular, jobs and news related blogs, which run parallel with native advertising, can generate a significant income. Native ads capture forty percent more attention due to their relevance and lead to higher click-through, and conversion rates, and eventually to a profits boost. No matter what device your audience uses, native ads automatically adjust to fit the size of the screen and always look great. Native Ad sites, which offer only quality content with a focus on relevancy, are Google AdSense, Outbrain, Mgid, and Taboola.

> ➢ Paid Reviews/ Sponsored Posts

Another excellent method of boosting your monthly earnings is through Paid Reviews. $10 or more can be easily generated from one small review related post. Recommended websites to look for paid reviews and sponsored content chances are Revcontent, Famebit (For YouTube channels), Tomoson, and Izea.

YouTube

On YouTube, you can connect with a community and have an opportunity to make money while doing what you love. Creators around the world have shared their voices on YouTube, and many have turned their passions into earnings. Creating a YouTube channel and getting thousands of subscribers - who does not like to make money while just speaking on camera, uploading, and sharing that video? Candidly all of this is too farfetched. The earnings of a YouTuber remains to be a polemical subject- few say they make a lot of money while some are always broke. In 2003, the Swedish YouTuber and comedian PewDiePie, earned $4 million thanks to the enormous number of subscribers to his YouTube channel. In the following year, the Swedish magazine Expressen reported that the production company 'PewDie Productions AB' made a profit of $7.5 million, most of which was from YouTube.

According to Statista, a statistics portal for market data and market analysis, the top 10 most popular YouTube channels as of September 2019, ranked by number of subscribers in millions, were: T-Series (110), PewDiePie (100), 5-Minute Crafts (60), Cocomelon–Nursery Rhymes (58), SET India (55), Canal KondZilla (51), WWE (47), JustinBieber (46), DudePerfect (45) and Badabun (42).

Exactly like any other business, this income option also demands initial funding or starting capital and some preparations and learning. Successful creators usually tap into multiple revenue streams to sustain their presence on the platform. Understanding the levers that impact monetization can help you plan your channel strategy to support your goals. With a dedicated audience that loves tuning into your channel, you can explore various ways to generate revenue, including from ads and other sources. Not just one, but there are many ways by which you can use YouTube for money-making. If you've been approved for the YouTube Partner Program and are in compliance with YouTube Partner Program policies, you can explore these monetization options.

Consider which revenue streams may be best for your channel based on your content, audience, and preferences.
- Ads
For many channels, advertising can be a significant part of revenue.
- Channel Memberships

With Channel Memberships, viewers pay a monthly recurring fee to get unique badges, new emoji, Members-only posts in the Community tab, and access to unique custom perks offered by creators.
• Merchandise
You can also earn revenue by selling merchandise that complements your channel. You can link to approved merchandise sites to offer your fans t-shirts, mugs, or other items.
• Brand deals
Working with brands can be another revenue stream and an opportunity to introduce new products and services to your audience.
• Super Chat
Super Chat is a way for fans and creators to interact in live chat. Fans can purchase Super Chats to highlight their messages within chat during a live stream.
• YouTube Premium
With YouTube Premium, viewers can enjoy videos on YouTube without ads while still supporting creators. It also lets viewers download videos to watch offline on mobile and play videos in the background.

Instagram

Globally, favorite Instagram influencers are making a serious amount of money from their clicked and shared pictures each day. Top Instagrammers make thousands of dollars with each post on this social media forum, people with an engaged follower list of around one thousand also have the money-making potential. And probably you looked down at your long list of followers and thought, "*If they can then I can, too.*"

Similar to bloggers, YouTubers, and other mediums where the crowd surrounds the people for the content they create, Instagrammers have uncovered the reach and persuasion- two top factors many firms struggle with. If placed together, these two components provide the Instagram influencers with a chance of scout for several paths for potential cashing. Whether you want to get access to some free services, make a little extra income, or create a steady revenue stream, it depends on your choice of strategy.

There are three major strategies to make money on Instagram.
1. Work as an influencer to post content sponsored by brands:
   Choose a niche, build trust, and grow your audience, partner with brands, and post transparently by making it clear when you are posting an ad, use the #ad hashtag above the fold.
2. Be an affiliate marketer selling other people's products:
   Choose a niche, find merchants to affiliate with directly or via an affiliate network, post about the product, be clear about the nature of your relationship with the product, and use the #ad hashtag.
3. Become an entrepreneur and sell your own products:
   This strategy goes beyond marketing and into the realm of actual eCommerce. Imagine your product, build your product, set up your account to make it shoppable, build out your eCommerce infrastructure, post your products, and of course, fulfill your orders.

Amazon KDP

Amazon Kindle Direct Publishing (KDP) gives individual authors the opportunity to publish their manuscripts as eBooks to be sold in Amazon's Kindle Shop and publish a paperback version of their book to be sold with a print-on-demand option over Amazon Books.

If you don't have any talent as an author or no time for writing a fiction or non-fiction book, then you have the freedom of hiring freelancers for content writing and publish the delivered manuscript under a pen name. After the freelance writer / ghost writer delivers the manuscript, you need first to make sure that the content is free from plagiarism, and does not have any grammar or typing errors.

The edited content requires formatting before publishing. This is done by tools provided by Amazon KDP. For Kindle eBooks, the manuscript is formatted and published by following these steps:
1) You start with the *Manuscript.doc* as a word file without headers, footers, and page numbers.
2) The tool 'Kindle Create' transforms the word file into a *Manuscript.kcb* file.
3) The tool 'Kindle Previewer' allows you to view how the eBook is displayed on Kindle and other mobile devices once it is published.
4) If the result is satisfactory, then the *Manuscript.kcb* can be published as a *Manuscript.kpf* file.
5) For publishing, authors need to upload the eBook cover (jpg, png) as well as the *Manuscript.kpf* into their bookshelf hosted by Kindle Direct Publishing.
6) Paperback versions of books can be uploaded as *Manuscript.pdf* files. The covers of paperbacks also have a spine and a back cover.

There are also other self-publishing sites, such as IngramSpark, but Amazon is the global market leader. Another advantage of Amazon is the possibility to advertise your books with Amazon PPC. If you manage to publish a certain number of books in eBook, paperback, and Audible formats, then you can count on a reliable passive income.

Freelancing

Most eCommerce market analysis and statistics point towards Freelancing as a great professional choice for making money online. According to research performed on behalf of the global freelancing platform UpWork in the upcoming ten years, more than fifty percent of the workforce in the USA will be freelancing, and forty-seven percent of Generation Z are already practicing it. An increasing number of people find freelance jobs adaptable, autonomous, and better way to earn more money.

But before jumping on this option, one must go through the drawbacks too. A high percentage of freelancers complain about not being able to find full-time regular jobs. They can't count on static and expected monthly income while undergoing a lack of perks from the employers. However, considering the large number and the variety of potential clients, generating a stable revenue is certainly difficult but not impossible.

The top freelance markets are Media Bistro, Upwork, PeoplePerHour, iWriter, 99designs, Designhill, Freelancer, Toptal, Simply Hired, Craigslist, Guru, Hubstaff, TaskRabbit, Speedlancer, LinkedIn, Bidvine, Fiverr, and Writing Gigs.

Airbnb

One of the best online markets for finding affordable and efficient vacation rental spots is Airbnb. As of 2019, Airbnb is reported to have over 150 million users and was last valued at $31 billion. There are listings in 191 countries around the world, with more than five million properties. That's more than the top five hotel brands combined!

After knowing about how you can start an Airbnb biz, you can note that they provide comfortable and handy lodging facilities for traveling. Another essential aspect to note is that it is a smart way to create returns in real estate. You don't need to be a homeowner or have access to a significant capital to get started with Airbnb, because the costs associated with listing your first property are pretty low. Plus, you can also use other people's properties.

Airbnb has a passive income system designed to use a living space for monetization. It creates relatively easy passive income earning by renting rooms, apartments, or even whole houses. Airbnb manages the reservations and bookings, the payments, and the rest belong to the responsibilities of the hosts.

There are three main ways by which you can earn with Airbnb, in which the first two are passive forms of income:
- You can lease out the properties you own.
- You can rent out someone else's property for a long duration (months, years) and then lease it out through Airbnb for shorter periods (days, weeks). This method is also called Airbnb Arbitrage.

Both of these options generate a steady passive income. If you go with the second option, then you need the approval of the landlord or the property owner before re-renting it for shorter periods, and you may or may not have the obligations of capital upfront. The third way of making money with Airbnb is called 'Side Hustle'.
- You can handle the real estate for landlords who wish to rent their properties on Airbnb.

Here is the basic outline and the necessary steps for getting your Airbnb business starting and developing:
  i. Setting Up Your Business
  ii. Building a Team
  iii. Market Research
  iv. Finding Properties
  v. Listing Your Property
  vi. Increasing Sales & Optimization
  vii. Automating Your Business

The above listed seven steps are intended to lead to business success if the following requirements can be fulfilled:

Research: Every geographical region draws in various kinds of travel enthusiasts-each of whom has different requirements. If you wish to know about their needs, then you can read your targeted region's Airbnb list. The list provides insight into the style and features of properties, price range, number of bedrooms, available extras, like AC.

Marketing your property: With enough information about your competition from the research you performed earlier, you can now modify and alter your listing professionally.

Title and Description: The rooms and apartments that are given for a short period should not just be bed and bath; they play a significant role in the user all-over experience. And this should be seen through the title and description of the property. Do not give all the details of the property. Make them realize the fun experience they have during their stay while simultaneously listing the advantages. This can also be used in elongating the property title. Search for useful and attractive property descriptions and tailor them to your own.

Pictures and Images: All uploaded photos should be authentic, distinct, good-quality, and in high definition. The picture quality increases by using natural light.

Airbnb SEO: Switch the instant-booking option to 'ON'. This adjustment makes the guest make a booking without conferring with the host. It seems that the Airbnb algorithm ranks the properties with instant-booking 'ON' higher. Stay should be set at a minimum of one night. Airbnb ranks such properties higher. Quick host response time. The quicker the host responds, the higher the ranking. Receive five-star ratings from your customers/tenants by knowing all about how to get high ratings, by over-providing on everything, and involving as many perks as you can, such as extra keys, toilet papers, towels, water, tea and coffee, milk, sugar, maps and guides for local attractions. You may also ask your guests politely to leave a five-star rating and mention you on their social media posts on Twitter and Facebook.

Turn your Airbnb into a passive income machine: It is necessary to manage the initial guests on your own; this way, you can adjust and refine your oblation. Though, once your system starts to function, it is time that you save your time and start outsourcing. Various turnkey companies in the market can assist you in turning your short duration rent outs into a trouble-free passive income stream.

Ramping it up: Once you know how to handle one rent out, you can start handling more than one.

OPTIMIZING YOUR ADS

The advertising technologies available today are providing marketers with more visibility than ever before. This transparency allows for more objective decisions to be made in real-time. The optimization of advertising campaigns is a continuous process; adjustments before, during, and after a campaign, ensure truly optimal results. There are several metrics you can use to measure the success of your ad campaigns; the most relevant metrics are: *cost per click* (CPC), *cost per thousand impressions* (CPM), *cost per acquisition* (CPA), *return on ad spend* (ROAS), *click through rate* (CTR), *conversion rate* and *average value order*.

Often these metrics are reported in combination with each other so that you get a clear picture of each campaign in comparison. This allows you to optimize the parameters of your campaigns accordingly. However, while these metrics give you the surface *return on investment* (ROI), which is vital for adaptive campaign management, the real metric of interest for every business owner is definitely the *net profit of each transaction* that's generated through the ad campaign. Understanding this allows you to make more informed decisions.

Amazon PPC

The first name that comes to mind when anyone says online shopping is Amazon. As per statistics, every month, around two-hundred million people make purchases on different Amazon marketplaces. People are busier than ever, and we live in a world that has been changed forever by the impact Amazon has made on home delivery of all manner of goods. Today's consumers want what they want at once, and they want it delivered fast.

Between 2015 and 2018, Amazon's ranking surpassed even Google in product searches. Today, Amazon owns a fifty-two percent share of the combined eCommerce markets of the USA, NAFTA, and Europe. The company also entertains market places in India, Japan, Australia, Brazil, and the tendency of growth continues.

However, China is a different story. Amazon has yet to crack the Chinese eCommerce market, which is without any doubt dominated by Alibaba, and it's several brands, such as Taobao, Tmall, and AliExpress. For example, Tmall has a market share of fifty-seven percent, while Amazon may call merely zero-point-eight percent of Chinese consumers as customers. There are reasons for this polarization, which mainly originate in the business models of the two companies, but the buying behavior of consumers also plays a role. Here are the key similarities and differences between Amazon and Alibaba

- Amazon and Alibaba are both eCommerce giants operating primarily without physical stores.
- Amazon dominates the American and European shopping spaces, while Alibaba does the same in China.

- Amazon sells products directly while also serving as an intermediary for other sellers, taking a cut of the sale.
- Alibaba charges merchants fees to appear higher on its search rankings.

Amazon, which can also be described as a giant retail platform, has provided a win-win situation to both the buyers and sellers. According to a report by Feedvisor, an optimization and intelligence platform for sellers on Amazon, in 2018, the professional merchants of Amazon have been able to secure a sales average of more than $ 1 million, which is a staggering one hundred percent more as compared to their sales in 2017. The monthly time spent on Amazon by Americans exceeds the time they spend on other top 10 eCommerce sites in total.

Pioneered by Yahoo in the late 1990s, the advertising philosophy based on PPC advanced since then immensely. Amazon has allowed sellers and vendors to advertise their products on Amazon since 2012, therefore making Amazon PPC (Pay Per Click) a reasonably young system in the timeline of PPC. This PPC program also opened the way to a support software industry. Tools for conducting keyword research, competitor analysis, ranking, and sales tracking, which are custom-tailored on Amazon FBA (Fulfillment by Amazon) and Amazon PPC, emerged to become necessary factors for success with Amazon. Jungle Scout, Helium 10, Viral Launch, AMZ Scout, and Ad Badger are the Top 5 of these tools. According to a January 2019 report by Ad Badger, the average cost per click (CPC) on Amazon PPC is $0.97. This amount is significantly higher at Google Ads ($2.76), Facebook Ads ($1.86), and Bing Ads ($3.36) and explains the popularity of Amazon PPC.

Here's the way Amazon maintains its uniqueness so that the search results display more of their ads.

1. Structure of the Campaign

In sponsored products, you need to establish an initial catalog campaign, as it would help you to begin your research for the perfect keywords, which are frequently entered by potential customers during their online shopping experience on different Amazon marketplaces. No matter if you have a few or many Stock Keeping Units (SKU), the catalog campaign would require all the products you have. PPC Advertising demands that all your products should be there in the catalog for representation. This leads to a better understanding of what terms and phrases have been used in the search process by potential customers. Until recently, the report on Amazon search term provided valuable data, which indicated the search terms that are precisely linked to the product SKU to the sellers through its data. Unfortunately, the update of the report done by Amazon no longer supports the data that can identify the search terms and its linked product.

The identification of relationships between the products and the search terms became difficult for sellers after the structural changes in Search Term Reports. For instance, the performance of root-keyword "toaster" is good, but this keyword cannot be matched up to any unique SKU. A possible solution for this problem is that only a single SKU should be added to a single ad group in the campaign structure. By this method, you would be able to conclude the success of SKU purchases and clicks directly through search terms. The solution of segmenting the campaign has a direct effect on the holistic success and, of course, the bidding strategy of the campaign. In simpler terms, more segmentation of campaigns would increase your control over products, and also it would increase your knowledge for investment decisions regarding products and keywords.

2. Keyword Harvesting

Your marketing strategy must include discovering the best keywords to increase search results for your products, and to increase your sales. The foremost objective of Amazon keyword harvesting is to find out the keywords that are often used by your customers and to make bids on them. You must bid for the correct keyword as enhances your products page sales rank along with the organic listing. All this would end up influencing and impacting the sales of your product.

Selecting the appropriate tools for keyword harvesting could be a tricky task. The third-party tools are undoubtedly efficient, but they are not functional when advertisers require raw information for strategical decisions and educated bidding. The primary source to utilize for keyword harvesting is the sponsored product's Search Term Report. It is available in Amazon Seller Central.

3. Refined Product Targeting

It is important to identify negative keywords to discover popular keywords and manage the costs of your PPC campaign. In case these keywords stay unnoticed without any solution, then you would be at risk of ad failure, which has been used for the terms that do not perform well, like limited conversions and less CTR.

The principal objective of negative keywords is to make sure that the search terms are relevant and refer to the products sellers are advertising for. It means sellers must put the relevant product in front of relevant search terms. Also, the negative keywords have to ensure that sellers do ignore keywords allocated spends that emphasize on creating clicks that do not convert. The identification of negative keywords can improve the performance of sponsored products ad campaigns. Also, the negative keywords enable the sellers to target a particular audience. You can achieve a more significant ROI if you start using negative keywords.

Google

Google is the most widely spread search engine and indeed the largest platform that has enabled advertisers to advertise their products through Google Ads (formerly known as Google AdWords), and grow their businesses by targeting new customer groups. In 2000, Google launched AdWords, a system where advertisers bid on keywords and pay when their ad is shown. In 2002, Google added its PPC system to its search results, using ad relevance to rank ads. In 2004, Google's US market share hit eighty-five percent, mostly from PPC advertising. Since the creation of PPC, Google has improved its relevance score.

Following Google's lead, Amazon, and the major social media sites like Twitter, Facebook, LinkedIn have also established their PPC systems. Over time, special PPC software has been created, and with the involvement of Artificial Intelligence, the PPC process is today in the hand of fully automated algorithms.

At the very first start, the optimization of Google Ads can be annoying, and most of the beginners are disappointed in their first campaign's paid search results. Google guarantees accessibility and ease of advertising, but when beginners do not optimize their ad campaigns appropriately, then the first results will surely be disappointing. The process of Google account optimization is much easier than one thinks. All you need is some preparation and planning, and along with that, one must obey some of the following best practices established by PPC.

❖ Google Ads Account Structure Optimization

Multiple elements can be optimized in the Google Ads; however, you need to focus on your ad account's structure as it is undoubtedly the most important one. There could be multiple issues with a poorly structured account. Some of these issues include lower quality scores, higher costs, irrelevant clicks, and much more.

The organization is the key to structure a Google Ads account optimally. Even if your account is already nicely positioned and enables you to approach new potential customers through your ads, still, if you spend some extra time on organizing the elements that create the structure of your Google paid search account, the outcome would be quite rewarding. In several ways, you can control the cost of your ads. Some of these ways include adjusting of various settings and targeting the account options.

The four key elements involved in the optimization of Google Ads account are: Campaigns, Ad Groups, Ads, and Keywords

❖ Negative Keywords

As explained under 'Amazon PPC Refined Product Targeting,' the negative keywords contradict their names; they are not the ones that have negative implications. Instead, they are the keywords that are not desired by an advertiser to appear in the searches made by potential customers.

For instance, you are the owner of a gardening supply store, and your first campaign is being planned. For this purpose, you would require to select keywords and make a bid on it. In this situation, you might think a keyword that has the word "garden" in it would be relevant. Well, not necessarily. Any keywords with the word "garden" in it may drive search results for a popular romantic comedy movie of 2004, *Garden State*. Or even bring results of music videos by *Savage Garden*, which was a pop band of the 90s. It may also bring results of the *Better Homes and Gardens Magazine*'s customer care department. All these search results are miles away from the products or tools of a garden supply store.

This hypothetical example explains that such keywords are required to be removed from your campaign, stating them as negative keywords. As the advertisers are required to pay some amount of money each time a person clicks on an ad, advertisers need to exclude such irrelevant keywords and search terms. Otherwise, their costs would increase without leading to any return.

❖   Targeting Parameters

The strength of Google Ads is, among others, the granularity, as it helps the advertisers to target potential customers. Although the potential of Google Ads requires attention and care for targeting options. They need to reach the right people in the correct place and at the correct time. The basic targeting option of Google Ads is keywords, but advertisers can implement other parameters also in their campaign.

Optimize Your Geolocation Settings:
The geolocation settings are the first targeting parameter that is optimized by Google Ads. Advertisers are allowed to refine the areas as per the display areas of their ads. Rather than meaning the position of ads on search pages, the display areas refer to the geographical location where the potential customers are at the moment when they conduct searches in the real world. For example, when consumers in Europe see ads for winter sports equipment and skiing resorts, consumers in Australia are confronted with sunscreen lotion and surfboard ads.

Optimize Your Dayparting Settings
Apart from the desired parameters of the location under Google Ads, you also get the chance to optimize the times and days during which you want the ads to be displayed in front of potential customers by customizing or adjusting the dayparting setting. The dayparting settings are available at the Campaign level through the Dimensions tab. For example, when consumers in Japan are shown restaurant ads with the best dining options in town, consumers in the USA get displayed juice and cereal ads for a healthy breakfast.

❖   Optimizing Text Ad and Landing Pages in Google Ads

The advertisers may face challenges while optimizing text, especially those advertisers who are engaged with large campaigns having multiple ad groups. To further complicate the matter, the optimization of ads should be done for both mobile and desktop campaigns, which further includes usable extensions. You must compare it to the daily business pressures, and you would understand why it is crucial for advertisers to optimize their text ads tightly. Several methods are there for creating an influential text ad, as well as advertising businesses in Google Ads. The best text ads share multiple qualities.
   ✓   The headline must contain a relevant keyword, at least once.
   ✓   The text ad must emphasize the unique selling point (USP) of your business, and the factor that motivates the potential customer to choose you over your competitor.
   ✓   An engrossing CTA (Call to Action) Click-Through Rate is required that initiates action and also establishes an expectation of what will happen after clicking on the ad.

Facebook

Digital ads provide access to millions of potential customers at a very affordable cost. In 2020, the traditional method of keyword targeting for finding customers is expected to be gradually replaced by audience targeting and audience segmentation.

By creating multiple audience segments, you can better create content custom-tailored to each audience's demographics, behavior, and specific interests.

You can win any battle if you have a good strategy, the same goes for the advertising on Facebook. As per the data, one-third of Facebook users are continuously interacting with at least a single business page of Facebook out of 60 million. While optimizing the Facebook ads, your target audience is the foremost important aspect of it. So how to identify your customers, and most importantly, how to analyze their desires and interests? Regularly, Facebook is engaged in extracting data from its ever-growing massive population of 2.07 billion users that you can find through audience insights. Audience insight is a free tool that enables you to grab information on your ideal customer. This would help you relate to your potential audience and develop better ads that could be optimized further accordingly. You can choose several parameters for targeting your audience on Facebook. It could be gender, relationship status, zip code or even hobbies. The statistic says the Facebook users are of ages between 18-49. But one can also actively look for the older audience on Facebook. Sixty-two percent of the '65 years and above' age group of the US population are found on Facebook. Facebook reportedly has forty percent higher senior users globally than any other social platform that persists.

Pioneered by Google, the complete process of digital ad campaigns is increasingly controlled and powered by machine learning and artificial intelligence systems. Amazon also adopted AI-powered PPC, leaving the control of their ad campaigns to the almighty Amazon algorithm.

Facebook does not yet offer these AI-features, but their new ad category called Dynamic Ads lifts the level of automatization to new heights. Using Dynamic Ads, all advertisers need to do is upload their list of products and set the time of their campaign. The rest is taken care of by Dynamic Ads, running in conjunction with the tracking code Facebook Pixel. Pixel is a tool that helps track purchases. The code is required to be installed in your website's backend to provide interaction among the Facebook ads and your website. Apart from tracing the website visitors, Facebook Pixel is capable of doing further nine more functions. It involves search, view content, add to wish list, add to cart, add payment info, initiate checkout, lead, purchase and complete registration. Based on the information provided by Pixel about conversion of the ads, and previous buying behavior of audiences, Facebook Dynamic Ads automatically display the right products to the right users, and potential customers. Due to the uniqueness of Facebook in terms of having access to a vast audience, PPC ads at Facebook have the ability of a multi-channel approach, namely via social ads and search ads. Customers who click on these two types of ads are more likely to convert than users who just click one type or the other.

Another powerful platform for ads is Facebook Messenger. The active monthly users of Facebook Messenger are 1.3 billion. Facebook Messenger is a different app dedicated to direct messaging purposes. According to the reports of Statista in January 2019, Messenger is the app with the most extensive demographic approach, as eighty-nine percent of the total population in the US between ages 25 and 34 regularly uses it. Since 2017, Facebook makes ad placements in Messenger, and enables your ads to get a higher reach by this unique placement opportunity. It has enabled brands to showcase them to their customers and also communicate directly with them. The response rates and conversions would increase as this ad placement would allow you to provide a personalized customer experience to your customer. You can choose from the given types of Facebook Messenger ads, which are Sponsored-Messenger Ad, Click-to-Messenger Ad, and Home-Screen Messenger Ad.

If you like to optimize your ads even more, then cross-channel marketing through the connection of your audiences both on Facebook (social) and Google (search) can be recommended. Search, and social are natural components. While a high percentage of shopping-related activities start with a search on Google, similarly, a considerable number of people use Facebook daily to socialize by visiting the platform and viewing videos. Cross-channel marketing campaigns, therefore, take paid ads to the next level. Among several good reasons why cross-channel marketing should be a key ingredient in your overall marketing strategy, the most striking is where stacking Facebook Insights, and Google Audiences are concerned. Together, they achieve a steep increase in marketing revenue and see the highest results from users.

New features of Facebook Ads also include Facebook Stories Ads (similar lime stories on Instagram), Facebook Augmented Reality Ads (allows users to virtually interact with products), and Facebook Playable Ads (allows users to try the game before buying).

Imagine a situation where your ad has been running for a few weeks, but you have not started gaining any returns out of it yet. Your audience is not at all showing interest in your ad, even though you have great creatives, amazing images, and a big marketing budget. Such a scenario would leave you with one factor, which doesn't seem correct, namely the audience. Targeting the correct audience is the most vital thing because the best of the campaigns and advertisements would not grab their attention if they are not interested in your product or service. You can optimize your target audience in different ways as offered by Facebook, here are the two most appropriate methods to do that:

❖   Retargeting

Once the learning phase of your ads is completed, and you finished analyzing the generated results, the phase of retargeting begins. The visitors who finalized their purchases or got converted at the first visit of your website are usually just two percent. You, therefore, need to grab the attention of these remaining ninety-eight percent potential customers. This goal is achieved through retargeting, also known as remarketing.

With the help of Facebook Pixel, a similar ad is displayed in front of those visitors who didn't get converted. Usually, showing a similar ad to an individual is done to remind them of your business. As per gained experience, the performance level of the retargeting ad set exceeds the performance of the target audience, although the requirements of both ad sets are important as they operate parallel to each other. It is because the audience who sees your first ad is also going to be retargeted again.

It is imperative to have high-quality photography of your products as up to ninety percent of an ad's success depends upon it. The visuals of your retargeting initiative must be new and fresh, so that customers may not get bored from a similar version repetitively. As the size of the retargeting audience seems to be smaller, a maximum of two to four variations in the text and graphics are enough. The metrics of Facebook involve the average frequency, determining how many times an ad has been shown to a person. For example, you can adjust the frequency of your ad so that it doesn't get displayed multiple times in front of the same particular customer.

❖   Lookalike Audiences

The Facebook Ads Manager enables you to create multiple custom audiences with distinct features like
-the people who are in your social media group
- or have interacted with you on social media,
-people who have visited your website,
-who have seen your videos,
-and the ones who are on the list of your customer emails.

The next step of target audience optimization is to develop a lookalike audience based on your custom audience. Your new audience is generated by a Facebook algorithm that uses the data of your prior custom audience. The data includes behaviors, demographics, and shared interests of your previous custom audiences. The counting of the custom audience recommended by Facebook should be in a range within 1000 to 50,000 people to create a reliable new list of lookalike audiences. The selection of behavior and features becomes difficult for the algorithm if this range is exceeded, and if the number is below the range, then sufficient data to generate a new audience list won't be available. The lookalike or similar audience ad sets do not require new original graphics as they are going to be presented in front of new viewers. One can ascertain that the performance of the lookalike audience and the custom audience are higher than the original target audience, but creating an original target audience is always necessary. Conversion of customers is only possible when the customers go through the sales funnel. The process of the sales funnel begins with creating awareness; hence you must use several audiences to achieve successful results.

In the context of the results, it is recommended to look for the end prize as it would help you optimize your ads properly by delivering them and optimizing them for success in the long term. You must ensure that your end goal should get benefitted through the metrics tracked by you. The essential metrics you must look for are the Website Conversion ROAS (Return on Advertising Spend), and the Website Conversion Value. Although, if you are tracking the registrations or operating-to-gain leads, you are also required to pay attention to click-through rates and link clicks. The optimization of your Facebook ad depends upon your progress, objectives, and continuous attention.

THRIVING ECOMMERCE MODELS

The past two decades have witnessed many eCommerce start-ups growing and declining. Monitoring the development of eCommerce trends, and thoroughly analyzing each trend in terms of potentially benefiting or possibly harming your existing business is a vital exercise. If failing to act accordingly, you might run the severe risk of falling drastically behind your competition. As we move into 2020, a bunch of new eCommerce trends are emerging, which are worth to keep an eye on.

The second-hand eCommerce, also called re-Commerce, is the rapidly growing online market for used products. The BOPS (buy online, pickup in store) option is increasingly offered in connection with fulfillment services. Pioneered by AliExpress, the use of Progressive Web Apps (PWA) is spreading to almost every eCommerce niche. Analyzing competitors' prices, reacting to seasonal demand, and adjusting their prices accordingly, needs to happen in almost real-time. Dynamic pricing is, therefore, essential for driving optimal sales and profit. The fast-fashion eCommerce industry is on the rise. Influencer endorsement and social sales combined with agility and speed play critical roles in fast-fashion. For being able to provide for the customers as they desire, and to engage with them, eCommerce businesses need to be present not only multi-device but also multi-platform. Conversational marketing, chatbots, and Artificial Intelligence (AI) are changing the eCommerce consumer experience for the better, and this trend is expected to continue in 2020 and beyond. And last, but not least, drone delivery is making rapid progress. Amazon and UPS are conducting experiments with drone delivery technology.

Below listed are six eCommerce Business Models that are currently blooming.

    1.   Private Label Products and Manufacturing

Many new eCommerce entrepreneurs come up with innovative product and service ideas but have no assets and capital to fund the product manufacturing on their own. Luckily, they have the option of importing products manufactured by other companies according to their ideas and then selling these products under their names and label. This business model is called Private Label Products. Several market forecasts and estimates point out that eCommerce merchandising with private labels is forecasted to quadruple until 2025 to satisfy the increasing demands.

There are advantages and of course, some disadvantages of private labeling. If the design is unique, then at least for a certain time, the owner of the patent, exclusive copyright, and distinctive design has a monopoly privilege in this particular market niche. Private labeled goods are created, branded, and traded for only one company, as long as the contract between the manufacturer and the eCommerce company remains valid. This situation makes the products of this brand unique and gives them a competitive advantage through differentiation from the competitors' products.

Combined with successful promotion and launch campaigns, private label products can formulate demand and define the market price. Products with separate tags generally relish with high-profit mark-ups. If they are the sole customer of the manufacturing company, the owners of the brand might gain control over the manufacturing and operation charges for minimizing the Cost of Goods Sold (COGS). Being the only distributor of such products, they can put high rate price-tags on these products - at least until counterfeit products with imitated design start emerging in this very same market niche.

Although these pros sound very promising, opting for private label business in eCommerce has also a few cons, barriers and risks. Looking for accurate private-label manufacturers to collaborate with is a challenge. Some entrepreneurs travel far and wide across the globe for developing nations like Vietnam. Other business-owners source the products from Chinese manufacturers via Alibaba, intending to reduce the cost-per-unit. Quality is vital for customer satisfaction and retention. With private labeled products, even if the prototype was found to be perfect, the manufacturers cannot ensure flawless batches. Hence quality control and storing an adequate number of products in inventory is imperative to dodge the costly customer complaint and after-sales service issues. Furthermore, selling branded goods through the internet that is produced and marketed by only one producer might restrict the consumers' reach.

2. White Labeling

The white label suppliers use their brand names to resell popular and prevalent products bought from any other third-party supplier. White labeling model works by charging the customer more for the branded, white labeled products than paying the manufacturing company for the goods.

White label suppliers can build their brand on white labeled products as well as create stronger relations with customers. White labeling may also boost their brand's visibility on the market. By selling white labeled products, one can add value to the goods by mixing and matching the offerings of different vendors. This method can optimize the white label suppliers' product line under the brand name.

One bottleneck that white label businesses go through is to handle inventory administration. Many of the retailers place a minimum quantity for the order to accomplish a considerable amount of savings by growing the production rates. Being a reseller, one should have good knowledge of their white label product demands. Maladministration of the inventory can leave white labels with vast batches of unsold stock or put them in a situation of not being able to satisfy the demand due to lack of products in the inventory, which eventually can lead to losing customers and market share.

3. Dropshipping

Lately, dropshipping has come up as a magical retailing performance model for all the eCommerce entrepreneurs who are starting their online trade companies with very little capital and zero assets. Dropshipping enables businesses to promote and trade products online without actually owning the products and stockpiling the inventory.

With the placement of orders, the dropshippers buy already sold goods from the suppliers; who in turn ship the products directly to the clients of the dropshipper.

These are substantial advantages of the dropshipping model:
- Dropshipping businesses don't have any expenses on warehouse and storage units, order or handle the stocks, pack and dispatch the product, check inventory or go through the returns.
- A dropshipping business venture can be started with no initial capital, continued with a limited budget, and then up-scaled over the time.
- Dropshippers don't need to hassle about manufacturing or inventory management, and completing the administration; they can invest their time and efforts in site designing, consumer support services, and promotion and marketing activities.

There are, of course, also come risks involved with dropshipping. Having no control over the product leaves dropshippers at the mercy of the manufacturers. If suppliers fail to deliver on time or ship low-quality products, then dropshippers certainly lose customers, reputation, and market share.

Dropshipping is not a passive income source. Even though the supplier handles the manufacturing and the delivery processes, the dropshipper can be hold responsible for all the delivery, shipment and tracking problems. One other risk is the robust competition, since online businesses according to this model are easy to start. This business model, therefore, should not be perceived as an unstressed eCommerce method; various intricacy levels should be attained.

4. Print-on-Demand

According to the Print-on-Demand model, the businesses trade with custom made designs printed on various products like t-shirts and other clothing materials, phone cases, mugs, etc. After the order is placed, the third-party producer prints the chosen pattern or image on the chosen product, packs the finished item into branded packaging material, and then ships the product on behalf of the eCommerce entrepreneur to the client straight away.

The benefits of print-on-demand models are similar to that of Dropshipping:

- Advance inclusion of funds is not needed, which makes it a low-risk model. These types of businesses only pay third-party producers after the finished products are shipped.
- Inventory and orders handling is kept in check by specialist third-party printing retailers like *Printify* and *Printful*.

To remain at the apex of this ever-growing marketplace, one must have a firm grip on graphic designing, know marketing strategies, and provide excellent consumer support. Some of the fastest expanding print-on-demand sites are *My Face Socks*, and the custom gift shop for pet lovers, *Lovimals*.

5. Subscription Services & Subscription Box Models

Think about it: you are sick and lying in bed with flu; you don't have the power to go grocery shopping; a food delivery facility that ships hot delicious soups and meals to your door front is exactly what you might need to fuel up. The charm and need for comfort and ease are what someone craves, and this has led to the emergence of a quick-developing subscription-facility in eCommerce models. One of the successful examples of the food subscription service provider is Healthy Surprise. Various other products that are provided on subscription bases are books, training, and videos, consumer goods that are subject to change at regular intervals, like electric toothbrushes, razor blades, and perfumes.

Subscription Services business model permits the clients to subscribe for a service for a limited duration of time; generally, it is for a month or a year. After the termination of this subscription period, the clients can -if they like - renew the membership and savor the convenience and achieve saving with every new order. What makes this eCommerce experience interesting for eCommerce owners are the following facts:
- They can upkeep consumer retention and fidelity by reducing the order withdrawal rates.
- They are allowed to prepare for delivery in advance and manage their inventory.
- They can luxuriate in low risks and high profits.

The pioneer in subscription for movies, shows, video games, and other forms of media is Netflix. In 1998 the startup company used to send subscribers physical copies of media, such as DVDs and CDs. Since 2015, the platform has advanced to streaming technologies that have elevated and improved Netflix's overall business structure and revenue. The platform provides its viewers the ability to stream and watch a variety of TV shows, movies, documentaries, and much more through means of using a software application.

From a consumer point of view, Subscription Box Models are one of the best ways to shop. This eCommerce model offers consumers unique experiences curated around products and themes, introduces new brands, and makes checking the mail just plain fun. On the business side, subscription commerce offers a stable financial model rooted in recurring monthly revenue, a reliable and steady stream of income that can be built around almost every niche – from puzzles to beauty to pets. If there is an existing community around a product or category online, chances are you can build a subscription box around it. You can also build up a list of subscriber contacts, which you can use to offer additional products or offer discounts in turn for getting their friends and contacts to subscribe, too.

According to the Forbes magazine, Birchbox deserves credit for beginning the subscription box movement back in 2010, delivering its care package of beauty samples for only $10 a month. Some of the most successful subscription boxes you may have heard of include Graze, Loot Box, Dollar Shave Club, Blue Apron. While these boxes can be shipped anywhere quickly and target a global market, subscription boxes can also target local markets, for example, weekly fresh deliveries of fruits, vegetables, eggs, and dairy products to nearby cities.

6. Wholesaling

Wholesaling resembles its name as it is a type of business in which products are sold in large quantities through an eCommerce platform at discounted rates. Generally, wholesaling is considered a business practice involving B2B transactions.

Wholesale eCommerce is a mostly automated process through implemented B2B online ordering software. Ordering software enables buyers, like retailers, to order products to resell from their suppliers, typically manufacturers or distributors, without having to use manual methods, such as calling, emailing, or faxing in orders.

The following offered features help you to distinguish reliable and profitable wholesale business partners from the numerous black sheep of this eCommerce market segment.
- Advanced wholesale eCommerce pricing
- Customer-specific wholesale eCommerce catalogs
- Easy wholesale eCommerce reordering
- Offline wholesale eCommerce ordering on mobile devices
- A native mobile app for wholesale eCommerce
- Barcode scanning
- Ability to review, modify, and confirm wholesale eCommerce orders

B2B workflows and business rules can be complicated, but they don't have to feel that way. If you manage to select the best wholesale eCommerce software for your business, then the system can replicate even your most complex workflows. This level of automation would enable a simple user experience for both your buyers, sales reps, and back-office staff.

CONCLUSIONS

Through eCommerce, international borders, and physical barriers are taken out of the equation when making a purchase. Nowadays, a single consumer in a small town somewhere in Montana can order for a single product from an Atlanta merchant and have it delivered by a supplier from Shanghai. It is easy to become a part of this new global, fast-changing, and exciting cyberspace of opportunities, called eCommerce.

Sooner or later, the correct eCommerce business model will surely bring you success, if you consider these essential aspects during your decision-making process: your capabilities, your budget and available capital, your short-, mid- and long-term goals, the identification of your target market, and of course, the selection of products and services you plan to offer.

Don't be afraid to lose a little money before you make it, consider these losses as an investment into building your eCommerce empire, starting with dynamic and optimized ad campaigns, and obtaining the necessary third-party software tools. Underutilizing what technology has to offer you would be one of the biggest mistakes you can commit when trying to establish your brand name. Pay attention to your product listings and your search engine optimization (SEO), so that the potential customers can find you on purpose, as opposed to by chance.

The author's intention for writing "ECommerce 2020 & Beyond" is to provide readers with an overview of the complete eCommerce landscape, which surely appears as highly complicated for beginners. After reading this book, you now have gained insight about all essential building blocks of this promising new industry. Understanding the basics is essential, but planning and innovation help you stand out and scale quickly in today's competitive eCommerce industry.

You must approach eCommerce with a single desire to not just win but to win decisively. For achieving this goal, the author wishes you good luck!

ABOUT THE AUTHOR

Marc Stanford holds a Master's degree in Advanced Computer Science and currently works on his Doctoral Thesis on Neural Networks. During his professional career, he is specialized, among others, in artificial intelligence and complex data modeling.

Although already experienced in tutoring and lecturing, writing technical books is Marc's newest passion. He lives and works in Palo Alto, CA, USA.

Also, by Marc Stanford

Programming with Python
An Easy to Understand Beginners Guide to Coding with Python

Non-fiction, eBook and paperback published in October 2019, ISBN-13: 9781696419642, available at Amazon in all marketplaces

Ethical Hacking
The Complete Beginners Guide to Basic Security and Penetration Testing

Non-fiction, eBook and paperback published in October 2019, ISBN-13: 9781698148427, available at Amazon in all marketplaces

The Age of AI
An Introduction to Big Data, Machine learning, and Neural Networks

Non-fiction, eBook and paperback published in October 2019, ISBN-13: 9781705603291, available at Amazon in all marketplaces